Windmills

Windmills

Laura Brooks

MetroBooks

LONGWOOD PUBLIC LIBRARY

MetroBooks

An Imprint of Friedman/Fairfax Publishers

©2000, 1999 by Friedman/Fairfax Publishers

All rights reserved. No part of this publication may be reproduced,
stored in a retrieval system, or transmitted, in any form or by
any means, electronic, mechanical, photocopying, recording, or
otherwise, without prior written permission from the publisher.

Library of Congress Cataloging-in-Publication Data available on request

ISBN 1-56799-756-2

Editor: Celeste Sollod
Art Director: Kevin Ullrich
Design: Robert Beards Design, Inc.
Photography Editor: Sarah Storey
Production Director: Karen Matsu Greenberg

Color separations by Fine Arts Repro Ltd.
Printed in Hong Kong by Midas Printing Ltd.

3 5 7 9 10 8 6 4 2

For bulk purchases and special sales, please contact:
Friedman/Fairfax Publishers
Attention: Sales Department
15 West 26th Street
New York, NY 10010
212/685-6610 FAX 212/685-1307

Visit our website:
http://www.metrobooks.com

There are, indeed, few merrier spectacles than that of many windmills bickering together in a fresh breeze in a woody country; their halting alacrity of movement, their pleasant business, making bread all day long with uncouth gesticulations, their air, gigantically human, as of a creature half alive, put a spirit of romance into the tamest landscape.

Robert Louis Stevenson

Contents

Blowing in the Wind

Whether you catch sight of it in a picturesque Dutch village, on a windswept American prairie, or along the rocky shores of the Greek islands, a lone windmill evokes the past. Standing tall, its face to the wind, it boasts sails that stretch out like strong arms embracing the elements.

A windmill is a machine that uses a wheel of slats or blades rotating in the wind to create energy. These versatile performers harness wind power to perform tasks ranging from generating electricity to grinding corn, crushing seeds, draining lakes, irrigating crops, and sawing wood.

In spite of its practical function, the windmill serves as much more than a workhorse. Throughout history, it has captured the imaginations of people around the world and transformed their everyday lives. Even today, to many eyes that have witnessed the technological wonders of the space age, windmills bear witness to the ingenuity of our ancestors and technological change. Their heritage spans the history of architecture, culture, science, and humanity.

In the past, the windmill was first and foremost a monument of civic pride. It dominated the landscape and was a source of collective identity for the community in which it stood. For the Dutch, the windmill was a national icon. Often it was the tallest structure in a village or town—even taller than church steeples—and it formed a beacon for residents and travelers. Early cartographers drew pictures of windmills on their maps as landmarks for navigating the countryside.

Since a single windmill might do the work of 250 people, it is not difficult to imagine how this machine dramatically improved people's lives in earlier cultures. Thanks to the wind-mill, a farmer who had previously eked out a living working the land could not only provide for his family, but also pump water to irrigate crops, grind more grain, and increase the volume of goods he brought to market. This great leap of efficiency made the windmill the basis of a new economy.

Page 8: *Some of the earliest windmills were constructed by the Moors of southern Spain in the early Middle Ages. These early mills may have influenced later examples, such as this one, from Consuegra, in the Spanish province of La Mancha.* Page 9: *The Tacumshane Windmill in County Wexford, Ireland, is typical of the small windmills that dot the countryside of Great Britain.* Right: *Tails like vectors turn the blades of these mills into the wind. Such simple yet ingenious inventions as tails characterize the history and development of windmills.*

On Faial Island in the Azores, Portuguese builders constructed these delightful contraptions.
Throughout history, millers have decorated their mills with bright colors, sayings, and pictures.

Milling Life

Wind is one of the oldest sources of energy for humankind. However, it is an erratic force, and unlike water, which can be controlled, it is harder to regulate. The fickle character of wind meant that the miller's job was a specialized skill. Millers had to take advantage of the wind when it arrived and might sometimes work for days and nights with no break while at other times, when the wind died down, be left with nothing to do. Windmills were low-tech but fussy instruments that required high maintenance, so a miller had to live on-site.

In Europe and the United States up to the nineteenth century, the miller was a high-ranking member of the small communities that depended on the productive potential of harnessing the wind. The miller was an important figure because he performed the essential function of grinding grains thus supporting the local economy. The miller was expected to be trustworthy and honest, and return to the customer the correct amount of ground grain. Inevitably, literature and folklore sometimes questioned the miller's character. As early as the Middle Ages, Geoffrey Chaucer described the corrupt miller of his *Canterbury Tales* in the following way:

> *His was a master hand at stealing grain.*
> *He felt it with his thumb and thus he knew*
> *Its quality and took three times his due.*

Most millers were reputable, however, and a community of up to one thousand residents or more might depend on the services of one miller. Townsfolk could also rely on the miller for up-to-the-minute news and the latest gossip because he

Mediterranean windmills are usually smaller than their counterparts in northern Europe. These windmills stand along a hillside overlooking Fatima, a village in Costa de Prata, Portugal.

interacted with nearly everyone in town. In the old days, people tethered their horses outside the mill, then brought their wheat inside to be ground. The cozy interior of the windmill must have provided the perfect environment for a chat. People both relied on and criticized the miller for his ability to forecast weather, much as we depend on, yet often dismiss, meteorologists today.

Millers felt a particular affection for their windmills and treated them as if they possessed individual personalities. Windmills were given funny names like Honey Vat, School Master, Pelican, The Maiden, The Empress, The Iron Hog, Abraham's Offering, and so on. Like ships, windmills were often decorated with carvings, paintings, and sayings or names. A fully bedecked windmill resembled a cherished dollhouse more than the practical machine that it was.

The famous story of Don Quixote, written by Miguel de Cervantes, has become inextricably linked with windmills. Here, Don Quixote is depicted with a post mill in the distant landscape.

Preserving Windmills

Windmills have captured the imaginations of writers and artists through the centuries. Ever since Miguel de Cervantes recounted how the dreamer Don Quixote "tilted at windmills," these landmarks have formed the basis of many stories. The French author Alphonse Daudet penned *Letters from My Mill*, a story about a miller of the nineteenth century. Leonardo da Vinci's sketchbook included drawings of many European windmills. Other artists such as Rembrandt—who was the son of a miller—have celebrated windmills on canvases that now hang in the major museums of the world.

After a period of decline and alarming destruction from the mid-1800s onward, great efforts were launched around the world to preserve windmills. All the countries of Europe boast windmill preservation societies, and some individual windmills have been restored to their original functions or converted into homes, shops, or restaurants. Many of them are still prominent local landmarks.

In addition to the windmill's historical value, many forward-thinking conservationists enthusiastically point to the windmill as an ecologically perfect device that offers a natural way to produce energy and preserve the earth's fossil fuels. In response, innovative windmills are being developed around the world. This renewed interest forms just the latest chapter in a centuries-old fascination with windmills.

Above: *By the seventeenth century, windmills like this one at Brill Hill, Oxfordshire, dotted the English countryside.* Opposite: *In Valentine, Nebraska, a wheat field stretches lazily at the feet of this wooden mill—an enduring symbol of the American Midwest.*

The tail pole was developed in order to make the job of turning the sails into the wind easier for the miller.
Many tail poles were equipped with wheels to facilitate hassle-free movement.

Form and Function

We're all familiar with the picturesque exterior of the windmill, but what goes on inside these wondrous machines? They may seem low-tech to modern eyes, but in earlier cultures, windmills replaced the labor of many people and provided a source of power never before dreamed possible.

Stepping inside a traditional European windmill is like stepping into a gigantic clock. After crossing the threshold of the low door, it takes a moment for your eyes to adjust to the dim interior. On quiet days, you can appreciate the array of pulleys, wheels, gears, and shafts that makes the windmill operate like a well-oiled machine. If the wind kicks up, you'll hear cracks and shudders as the sails begin to turn, culminating in the loud whirring sound of the arms, which can travel up to thirty miles (48km) an hour at their tips. On windy days, you'll be greeted by a cacophony of noises—the clucking of gears, the grating of the millstones, and the rush of the grain as it funnels into great wooden bins.

Parts of the Windmill

Over time, windmills have been adapted to perform specialized tasks, from hulling or pressing oil from seed, to sawing wood and milling many other

kinds of coarse materials. Windmills, therefore, are as individual as their builders and applications, and it is hard to generalize their functional components. However, traditional windmills share certain basic features.

First, traditional, European-style windmills usually stand at least three stories high, and the average Dutch windmill has five or six levels. The ground level forms the miller's workspace, which in the past often doubled as a living area for the miller and his family. The first level also serves as grain storage. The second floor contains the millstones, and the third story contains the hoppers into which grain is poured. In the cap, the top part of the windmill, are the wheel and windshaft, which are connected to the sails outside the windmill.

The focal point of the windmill's interior is the one or more millstones for grinding grain. The lower millstone is referred to as the bed stone, which usually remains stationary. The upper or runner stone rotates or revolves above the bed stone. Millstones have grooved surfaces and the distance between the two stones can be adjusted according to the desired fineness of the final product. A lever, or even something as small as a screw, can be used to regulate the fineness of the grain.

The miller built his reputation on his skill at adjusting the millstones to produce the highest-quality product. Since millstones were the financial centerpieces for the miller and his windmill, they were painstakingly maintained. Stones had to be dressed or regrooved periodically, and each miller had his own way of dressing the stones in order to get the most out of the grain. The miller used a hammer and chisel to carve one-of-a-kind grooves for a custom job. Each stone was unique and the

Above: *American ingenuity was responsible for this homemade contraption—a windmill used to power the owner's circular saw. For the clever farmer, the mill facilitates cutting a year's supply of firewood.*
Opposite: *The white windmills of the Mediterranean, including this one on Karpathos, in the Dodecanese islands of Greece, stand in stark contrast to a sapphire-blue sea.*

number of grooves, the profiles, and the carving techniques were carefully guarded trade secrets.

A variety of gears or other interlocking equipment connected the millstones to the sails. The windshaft linked the sails to the internal machinery, so it had to be made of strong wood or metal, and it was usually chiseled into an octagonal or round profile. The end of the windshaft was fitted into the brake wheel, a huge wheel that measured up to ten feet (3m) in diam-

Above left: *Windmills require regular maintenance, and throughout history, millers have constantly made adjustments to ensure that their mills run as well-oiled machines. This 1879 woodcut depicts the maintenance of the Old Mill, built in 1746, on the island of Nantucket in Massachusetts. The massive windshaft withstood the force of the winds.* Above right: *After being ground by the mill-stone, the grain tumbled down a shoot to a waiting sack to be bagged and given to the customer.*

eter. Gear teeth around the rim drove a stone nut, which in turn drove the millstones. The brake put the brake wheel into action to stop the turning motion of the sails. The brake was operated by a lever or rope and clamped down over a large section of the brake wheel to stop its movement. In very windy conditions, the miller had to exert all his strength on the brake lever to stop the movement of the mill.

A hoist made of a long chain or rope lifted grain sacks into the hopper above the millstones, where grain would be fed through the system. Meal bins held the grain, and a shaking tray called the "miller's damsel" regulated the flow of grain into the grinding stones. The ground grain poured out into large bins on the floor level, where it was bagged and then removed from the windmill.

The sails, usually made of cloth, were stretched across lattice frames rotating on an axle. The farther out the fabric was stretched, the faster the grindstones turned. Most windmills had four sails, though it is not unusual to find mills with as many as eight or as few as two. The sails were usually curved like the wings of an airplane or tilted slightly to catch the wind. Each

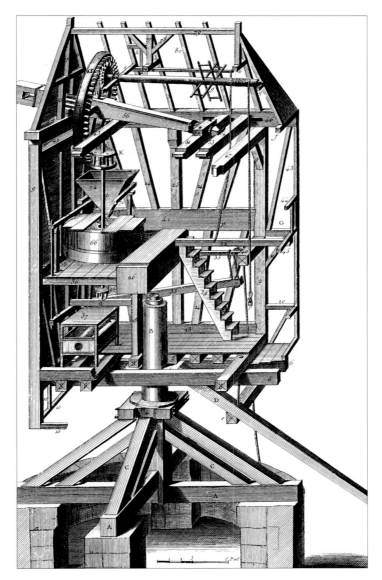

An interior view of a post mill clearly depicts its mechanical parts. This mill was used for grinding grain, which was fed into a hopper on the upper level. The grain spilled into the grindstone, and the ground kernels were then bagged.

arm measured from twenty to sixty feet (6m to 18m) long and usually rotated in a counterclockwise direction.

The sails had to be able to turn into the wind as it shifted so that no matter what the wind direction, the mill could continue to operate. Windmill builders solved this challenge in a number of ways. In post mills (see page 22), the entire boxlike body of the mill rotated into the wind. In tower mills (see page 22), only the cap turned toward the wind. Some windmills had a fantail, an invention of the mid-1700s that kept the sails ever pointed in the windward direction. The fantail was fitted with a

tail pole hanging toward the ground. In order to change the position of the sails, the miller simply pushed the tail pole in the proper direction.

An elaborate vocabulary developed to describe different parts of windmills. Historically, many of the parts of the mill were called by feminine terms. The outside stone body of the mill was called the skirt, the center part was the waist, and the grinding surface was referred to as the dressing. For example, a cry from the miller to his assistant—"Don't choke her eye!"—indicated that the wheat should not be fed into the hopper too quickly.

Types of Windmills

The earliest type of windmill in western Europe was the post mill, known from the twelfth century onward in Germany, England, and France. The post mill was a top-heavy unit with sails that revolved around a single post at its base. The upper part of the mill consisted of a boxlike body that contained the millstones, gears, and shaft for supporting the sails. Four to six sails of wood or canvas were stretched across frames. A small fan served as a rudder to keep the windmill facing in the windward direction. Although colonial America boasted many post mills, only the Robertson Mill in Williamsburg, Virginia, offers contemporary viewers an idea of how these structures must have appeared to the early settlers.

A second type of windmill, the tower windmill, is familiar to anyone who has visited Holland. The large tower was constructed of wood, brick, or stone and was topped by a timber or thatched roof. Its form was fully developed by the fifteenth century. In contrast to the post mill, on the tower mill, only the cap with its sails revolves, not the entire body of the mill.

The "smock" mill was so named, according to tradition, because it resembled a person wearing a smock. An alternative to the tower mill, it was usually framed in wood and covered with boards in an octagonal design, which gave it the appearance of a giant figure wearing a smock or dress.

There are many variations of these basic types of windmills, and in Holland, a vast vocabulary developed to describe windmills that performed specific functions. In addition, specialized windmills developed in particular regions. In North and South

Above: *At Darling Lake, in Nova Scotia, Canada, a windmill towers over the carriages and trees in the vicinity. Before skyscrapers, windmills were often the tallest structures for miles around. They were at least as high as many church steeples and formed unique landmarks for townsfolk and travelers.*
Opposite: *The picturesque quality of windmills captures the imaginations of people around the world. Each one is a unique creation.*

America and Australia, for example, the skeletal appearance of the metal-framed mill dominates the landscape. In Africa and Asia, horizontal mills—probably the earliest examples of windmills in the world—provide a fascinating alternative.

Technological Windfalls

Through the centuries, inventors, engineers, architects, millers, and dreamers have devised ingenious additions and changes that have improved the windmill's function. With the design of a cap that turned the sails to the wind, for example, people no longer had to turn the entire box of a post mill. In the eighteenth century in England, inventor Edmund Lee placed a tail with a wheel on the opposite side of the tower from the sails, which had the effect of turning the mill automatically in the direction of the wind. Governors, or belt-driven weights, were eventually developed to adjust the space between the millstones mechanically by controlling the opening and closing of the slats and, therefore, the speed of the sails.

In 1772, Scottish millwright Andrew Meikle invented the spring sail, which in part solved the problem of furling and unfurling sails in windy weather, a process that proved dangerous and even fatal for some millers. In Meikle's design, the arms of the mill were fitted with wooden shutters connected with a bar not unlike that on venetian blinds. These were regulated with a tension spring, which caused the blades to open and close with the strength of the wind. When the wind was light, the shutters closed to make the maximum use of the available wind. When the wind was heavy, the shutters opened to regulate the speed of the sails.

Above: *This print depicts a design for a Dutch windmill used for pumping water. The windshaft operates a water wheel on the lowest level. The Dutch became known for their ability to drain enormous bodies of water using the power of windmills.* Opposite: *The Mojave Desert in southern California presents a stark yet sublime landscape. Windmills serve as towering monuments across these flatlands and provide much-needed water for this arid region. Note the short fantail, designed to turn the sails into the wind.*

Another improvement was initiated in 1807 by Sir William Cubitt, who invented self-reefing sails. In this design, the movement of the shutters could be controlled by a weight suspended outside the mill. The advantage was that the miller did not have to stop work in order to adjust the sails; the adjustments could be made while the sails were turning. Once steam and electrical power came into use, windmills seemed doomed. But it wasn't long before ecologists and others interested in energy conservation looked back to the windmill as the future of power and energy. Today, new windmill innovations continue to be developed around the world.

A Day in the Life of the Miller

Throughout history, the miller's job has been like that of a captain piloting a large sailing ship. The miller has constantly monitored weather conditions, understood the meaning of cloud formations and shifts in humidity for his business, and orchestrated a complex symphony involving man and machine. Historically, most millers have been men, though couples sometimes worked together as a team, and widows of millers are well documented throughout history as having taken over their husbands' businesses.

The life of the miller was unpredictable. He had to work when the wind blew, so his daily regimen was as change-able as the weather. He might work for days in a row without sleeping, then stop work for a week if the weather was calm. Some millers even tied tin cups to the mill's sails so that they would be roused if the wind picked up while they were sleeping.

It was an active life, as the miller had to climb up and down the stairs of the windmill constantly—up to make sure the grain was feeding from the hopper correctly, down to inspect the millstones and the finished product. The inside of

the mill, as well as the miller himself, must have stayed flour-coated. The reputation of the miller was built in part on how well he could adjust the distance between the millstones to achieve the desired quality or fineness of the milled grain. This was a perpetual challenge, as the speed of the wind made the space between the stones vary.

It was a dangerous job. The great height of many windmills and their need for regular maintenance made the miller's job particularly risky. In the early days of the windmill, the miller had to take the sails in by hand as a storm was brewing, the cloth drawn in from each arm. After the storm passed, the miller then had to replace the sails on their frames.

The miller's greatest fear was that the millstones would continue to turn once all the grain had been ground. If the miller did not stop the sails just as the grain was finished, the wind would cause the stones to grind against one another, creating sparks that might set the shaft on fire and send the entire windmill up in flames. Therefore, the miller had to know exactly when to furl and unfurl the sails to catch the wind at the right time. Windmills were equipped with a brake that would halt the sails long enough for the miller to climb to the top and unfurl the cloth. But if the wind was already too strong, it might overtake the strength of the brake and send the sails turning. Uncontrollable shaking of the mill and sails was another danger, and the miller might have to ride out the storm like a veteran sailor.

Western France is dotted with solid windmills constructed of stone which provided sturdy homes and workplaces for the millers and their families. These monuments celebrate the rugged simplicity of French vernacular architecture.

Windmills weren't invented in Holland, but they came to serve as a national icon for this small country.
Any resident or visitor will tell you that they account for the unique character of the Dutch landscape.

Windmills in History

No one knows exactly when or where the first windmill was built. According to tradition, the Babylonian leader Hammurabi used windmills to irrigate crops in the twentieth century B.C., but of course, evidence of such mills has long disappeared. However, ancient civilizations surely understood the power of the wind as an energy source. Fragments of pottery and wall paintings from ancient Egypt show boats with sails using the wind to navigate the Nile.

Before windmills came into common use, early farmers irrigated their crops by carrying containers of water out to the fields. The small amount of grain the farmers could harvest was ground into meal using primitive tools and rocks. The ancient Greeks and Romans used water wheels to turn millstones for grinding grain. By about the first century A.D., a device known as a *quern* was invented to facilitate grinding. Grain was poured into a hold, where it was ground with a smooth rock fitted with a hollow stone.

Water seems to have been used more readily than wind to accomplish laborious tasks in early cultures. However, water was not available everywhere, and low, flat, sandy areas that were naturally breezy lent themselves to harnessing the wind as a source of energy. Therefore, it is not

Above: *We can only speculate about the appearance of windmills before the Middle Ages. However, documents from ancient Greece and Rome describe the presence of wind machines, which may have looked something like the one of circa 150 B.C. reconstructed here.* Right: *The earliest American windmills were constructed of wood, but metal would soon reign as their primary material. Windmills were mass-produced in the Midwest by the mid-nineteenth century.* Opposite: *The earliest type of European windmill was the post mill, which consists of a stationary base with a revolving upper body. Post mills could be found across northern Europe by the twelfth century.*

surprising that the arid deserts of the Middle East formed the cradle of the windmill.

Ancient Beginnings

The earliest documented windmills are from Seistan, Persia, in modern-day Iran. A millwright is attested to being there as early as 644 A.D., and windmills were recorded by Arab historians and geographers in the tenth century. In his encyclopedic work *Meadows of Gold and Mines of Precious Stones*, the historian Masudi described wondrous engines that ground grain. Locals told him these mills were very old and that an Egyptian warrior had introduced the idea in Persia during the time of Moses. Masudi also described how mills were used to pump water to irrigate the luxurious gardens in the region. In 947, he wrote,

"…wind turns mills which pump water from wells to irrigate the gardens. There is no place on earth where people make more use of the wind." In 1283, al-Qazwini, a Persian scholar, told how mills in the area not only pumped water, but ground corn and even redistributed the drifting sands that would climb so high as to envelop habitations if not evenly dispersed.

The windmills described by these early historians—some of which still exist—are fundamentally different from the upright mills that later populated the Western world. The Middle Eastern windmills are horizontal rather than vertical, with sails radiating outward from a central vertical post. The sails are encased in a

Above: *Engineers, architects, and dreamers have developed unique windmill creations throughout the centuries. This wheel windmill, in which the sails turned horizontally rather than vertically, was designed around 1719. Horizontal windmills have operated in Asia and the Middle East since ancient times.* Left: *Windmills have also served the small communities on the Greek island of Crete since antiquity.*

stone or adobe construction, with openings carved to funnel the wind, causing the sails to turn.

Other examples of the world's oldest windmills survive in Afghanistan, a country with no seacoast or navigable rivers, but with many high mountains with windy conditions. The windmills there are closely linked to those known in Seistan so many centuries ago. In this type of windmill, the millstones lie above the sails, which are turned around a central vertical pole by wind rushing through slats cut into the sides of the adobe building that houses them. Later, the sails were placed above the millstones.

Other early windmills come from China, where they have been used for centuries to irrigate crops. The horizontal contraptions are thought to have been modeled on those of the Middle East, and some historians think that the earliest ones may even have been designed by Persian millwrights captured by the

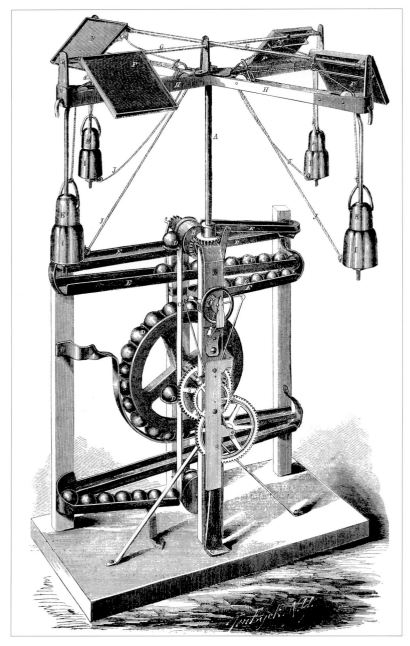

By the seventeenth and eighteenth centuries, windmill designs such as this one were widely printed and disseminated in books. In this way, European windmill designers shared ideas, both experimental and practical.

troops of Genghis Khan. In inner Mongolia, windmills are still used to generate electrical power for nomadic peoples, and approximately two thousand of these structures exist.

In contrast to the sails of the Middle Eastern mills, which are encased inside buildings, the sails of Chinese windmills are usually freestanding. These are the most lightweight windmills, often constructed of bamboo poles with sails of thin cloth or matting. These one-level structures resemble delicate merry-go-

In an 1886 painting entitled "Tulip Field in Holland," the French Impressionist painter Claude Monet depicts the ever-changing effects of light and color on the Dutch countryside; the windmill was an integral part of the scene, even then.

Above: *This picturesque windmill—as well as its pastoral surroundings—in Quainton, Buckinghamshire, England, evokes the history of the region.*
Opposite: *These windmills in southern Holland line up like soldiers determined to execute their task. Windmills like these were constructed all over the country in order to transform Holland's swamps and wetlands into plots of land that were livable and agriculturally productive.*

rounds, with triangular jib sails that bring to mind Chinese sailing vessels. The horizontal Chinese mills, with sails revolving parallel to the ground, have the advantage of not needing to be turned toward the wind, as is the case with upright mills. The sails sit in a fixed position, set obliquely to the wind so that the wind always blows one part of at least one sail. The disadvantage of this design is that only one or two sails at a time catch the wind. Therefore, these mills are less efficient and less powerful than the upright mills.

The Middle Ages

The origins of the upright windmill, which dominated the countryside of Europe by the seventeenth century, are nearly as obscure as those of the mills of Iran. Was the form borrowed from the East? Did the Europeans invent it independently? Or was it based on an ancient prototype of which no example survives?

Some speculate that the idea of windmills may have been transported to Europe in the footsteps of the Crusaders, who traveled via inland and water routes to the Holy Land on vari-

From early on, many designers incorporated a platform around the great girth of the windmill. This structure facilitated the furling and unfurling of the canvas sails, a task which might otherwise prove more difficult for the miller.

Just as a lighthouse keeper's existence centered on the lighthouse, the lives of millers and their families revolved around the windmill. Therefore, living quarters were usually constructed inside or adjacent to the mill's tower.

ous military campaigns throughout the Middle Ages. Some Crusaders described windmills they saw on the Greek islands of Rhodes, Mykonos, and Tenedos. By the fourteenth century, the great number of windmills in the harbor of Rhodes—where the legendary Colossus of Rhodes had stood in ancient times— earned it the name Harbor of Windmills.

Though standing examples of windmills before the Middle Ages are unknown in Europe, legends about these mysterious and wonderful contraptions abound in folklore. According to one story from Ireland, a third-century king, Cormac Ulfada, fell in love with the Princess Ciarnute. When his wife, the queen, learned of her husband's infidelity, she sentenced the princess to labor all day long grinding corn. When the princess begged the

king to relieve her from this toil, he sent for a workman in Scotland to make an engine—a windmill—to grind the corn.

Whether or not the Crusaders were responsible for transporting the idea of windmills to Western Europe, by the twelfth century these contraptions were referred to as Turkish mills, perhaps suggesting an eastern origin. By this time, windmills were commonplace in Europe. One is cited in 1105 in Arles, in southern France; another in Normandy in 1180. In England, too, windmills had become part of the landscape by the twelfth century. They were familiar landmarks by the end of the Middle Ages in Holland, England, France, and Germany.

In medieval Europe, windmills meant power, and only wealthy landowners possessed them. Mills were the prerogative

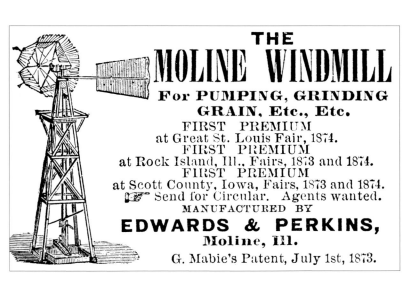

Above: *In the nineteenth and early twentieth centuries, American agricultural journals and local newspapers regularly advertised windmills. Chicago formed the windmill manufacturing hub during the heyday of windmill sales.* Opposite: *Historically, canvas windmill sails had to be furled and unfurled by hand, a laborious process that required great strength and skill.*

of powerful lords, who maintained the right to use them, permit or refuse access to them, and reap profits from them. Windmills stood at the center of legal battles. For example, the monks of the abbey of Windsheim in Holland wanted to erect a windmill at Zwoll, but the lord in their region claimed rights to the wind in that district. The monks appealed to the Bishop of Utrecht, who granted windmill-building rights to the monks. A windmill could also provide a safe haven or lookout in this insecure time. During the battle of Crécy in 1346, the English king Edward III climbed the tower of a stone windmill with walls seven feet (2m) thick and used it as an observation post.

Medieval builders designed the post mill, which was strong enough to resist winds but light enough to spin easily in the breeze and to allow a person to turn the sails toward the wind. Often such a mill was supported by tree trunks or a strong tripod. The box was just large enough for a man to sit inside and work.

The Windmill Heyday and New Horizons

From the twelfth through the eighteenth centuries, windmills spread all over western and central Europe and Scandinavia. The windmill evolved from the post type to larger models, the tower and smock mills. Working drawings of these machines were widely published and circulated in France and Holland by the early 1700s—the heyday of the windmill.

The development of steam power, the internal-combustion engine, and electricity outmoded windmills, and their numbers began to decline dramatically from the late nineteenth century onward. In Hungary, the hard wheat that grew was unsuited for traditional milling and could not be ground into fine grain. Inventors in that country began experimenting with steam power and applying it to milling as early as 1820. The idea soon spread throughout Europe and the United States, and steam

Above: *The smock mill was so named because onlookers thought this type of mill resembled a giant person wearing a smock. Smock mills are usually six- or eight-sided.* Left: *A weather-beaten barn and accompanying windmill remain as testimony to the self-sufficiency and ingenuity of American farmers of the nineteenth and early twentieth centuries.* Pages 46-47: *The historic windmill in East Hampton, on Long Island, New York, stands among the country's oldest structures. The form of the tower mill pays homage to Europe, but its weathered gray shingle siding brands it as colonial American.*

engines threatened to make the windmills obsolete. Soon windmills went untended, the sails rotted, mice and birds moved inside, and moss grew on the cold stones.

However, the windmill wasn't completely doomed. By World War I, homes across the United States were fitted with small, two-bladed windmills that could be mounted on the roof of a house in order to generate enough power to operate a radio. This design was improved through the 1930s and 1940s. Many other designs and innovations characterize the history of windmills, and today, engineers around the globe continue to create chapters in the history of this ancient tool.

*Dawn in southern Holland: windmills line the edge of a dike against a spectacular display of color
on the horizon. Many windmills were needed to control the sea and lakes of this tiny, water-logged nation.*

A Nation of Windmills

When the word "Holland" is uttered, the image of a windmill springs to mind. Windmills were not invented in Holland and appeared there only around 1200 A.D. But the development and economic success of this tiny nation would not have been possible without the work of windmills. René Descartes coined the now-popular saying, "God made the world, but the Dutch made Holland." Windmills made it all possible.

Until the late Middle Ages, the region later known as Holland was practically unfit for human habitation. The Lowlands, or Netherlands, were just that—low-lying marshes, bogs, lakes, and sand dunes, all of which flooded from time to time with the rushing in of the sea. In the first century A.D., Pliny reported that the region's few inhabitants lived on wet mounds surrounded by water. Flood was a constant threat.

Once windmills appeared in the area by the end of the twelfth century, however, people quickly realized that the machines could be used to pump water and regulate flooding. By the 1400s, windmills drained water into newly built canals all over the region. Each mill had a revolving scoop that rested on the ground. The wind lifted the scoop into the air, and the water would be dumped into a ditch or canal on higher ground.

Dutch windmills are larger than their counterparts elsewhere in the world. On average, they measure about ninety feet (27m) in diameter at the base and stand at least three stories high.

Windmills have been constructed of many materials, including brick, wood, stone, and plaster. In the eighteenth century, the Dutch imported strong Douglas fir trees from North America in order to construct unbreakable windshafts.

Some two million acres (808,000ha) were drained and made habitable in this manner. Windmills turned flooded, stagnant bogs into fertile tracts of land called *polders*. Polders are sections of land surrounded by high earthen walls that keep the water out. Windmills, sometimes mounted on the turrets of city walls, pumped water and dumped it into troughs, keeping the polders dry. Eventually, the water formed streams that returned to the sea. This impressive system was not perfect, however. Even after windmills helped tame the North Sea, seventy-two people from the village of St. Elizabeth perished in 1421 when they were washed out into its cold waters.

By the seventeenth century, however, windmills had drained numerous lakes across Holland, making the land not only habitable but also economically prosperous and visually striking. Holland is essentially flat, so windmills, rising above all other buildings, have become a symbol of that country.

The ingenious Dutch also used windmills for hulling rice; pressing oil from seeds; sawing wood; pulverizing grain, raw materials for dyes, and limestone; and performing other tasks that supported a burgeoning economy. Pretty soon, everybody depended on windmills, either directly or indirectly, for a living. Exotic goods brought back from Dutch colonies in the West Indies, including spices, cocoa, rice, barley, tobacco, and other items, were processed in windmills at home and in newly erected ones in the Dutch colonies of the Caribbean.

Dutch windmills are larger than most other windmills in the world, measuring an average of ninety feet (27m) in diameter at the base. The Dutch enlarged this space on the ground level in order for the miller and his family to live inside the great machine. In spite of the mill's large size, living space was secondary to work space, so quarters were cramped and beds were sometimes built into the walls.

Among the Dutch innovations was a windmill in which the upper cap revolved, obviating the need to turn the entire turret.

Above: *An optical illusion: these windmills are clever miniature versions of the ubiquitous monuments of Holland. They form part of an exhibit in the Madurodam Miniature Park in the Hague.*

At sunset in Schemerhorn, Holland, the silhouette of a grand windmill offers a breathtaking view for visitors and residents.

Above: *In traditional Dutch windmills, the miller must furl and unfurl the sails by hand before starting and after stopping the motion of the mill. This grueling work might also prove risky if the wind is unpredictably strong.* Right: *Fishing boats and windmills form an integral part of this panoramic countryside near the Hague. Scenes such as this have inspired countless landscape painters.*

The cap could easily be rotated from within the building using a beam mounted on a circular track. Some of the wood used to build Dutch windmills was shipped to Holland from America in the eighteenth century, including Douglas fir, an especially hard wood. Fire was a constant threat, as many of the early roofs were thatched; and as the highest structures around, some windmills naturally attracted lightning. Sometimes wood had to be salvaged from a burning windmill in order to build a new one.

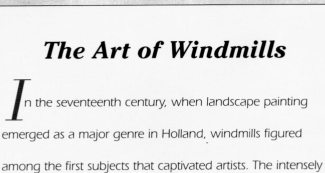

The Art of Windmills

*I*n the seventeenth century, when landscape painting emerged as a major genre in Holland, windmills figured among the first subjects that captivated artists. The intensely naturalistic, picturesque scenes portrayed the pride of the Dutch people for their land and the beauty of the country.

Some of the major painters of the period—Rembrandt van Rijn, Jacob van Ruiidael, Jan van Goyen, and others—focused on the windmill as a central theme in their work. For some artists, the windmill was more than simply a picturesque subject. Rembrandt van Rijn was the son of a miller, and his name, van Rijn, derived from the name of his father's windmill in Leiden.

In this nineteenth-century painting by Charles H. J. Leickert, the artist pays homage to the centrality of the windmill in the Dutch landscape. The windmill formed a favorite subject for artists in Holland, England, and elsewhere long past the seventeenth century.

Above: At the Zaanse Schans Museum near Zaandijk, Holland, visitors get a firsthand look at the operation of a historic windmill.
Opposite: At sunrise in Stompwijk, Holland, the vivid light creates a reflection of windmills in the canal.
Scenes such as this stand as reminders of Holland's impressive windmill heritage.

Types of Dutch Windmills

The Dutch invented a staggering array of specialized windmills—most being variations of the tower mill—each with its own name, terminology, and specialized function. These machines ranged from small contraptions meant to drain ditches to very large multistoried mills that doubled as homes for the millers' families.

The *standermolen*, a type of post mill and the oldest type of windmill in Holland, is most common in the southern region of this low-lying country. The hollow post mill, or *wipmolen*, served mainly as a drainage mill and used hollow posts in order to draw up water and discharge it through its upper end. The charming wipmolen usually had a thatched, cubic house alongside it.

The larger drainage or polder mill, called a *bovenkruier* in Dutch, was a more powerful machine used to drain the land. This type of mill appeared in the sixteenth century in the wetter, northern part of Holland. It is usually octagonal and brick with a movable cap. A scoop wheel was used to collect water in shallow places, and a water screw drew it up in deeper water. Many of these mills were located along canals and lakes.

Other specialized drainage mills included the *binnenkruier*, a tower mill with a rotating cap found primarily in northern Holland. The *stellingmolen* was a tall tower that often occupied the ramparts of a city wall and sometimes had a stage built around its circumference to make furling and unfurling the sails easier for the miller. There were also many other smaller varieties of windmills, each with its own name and particular function.

Preservation Efforts

The use of steam power to drain Haarlem Lake in 1848-52 seemed to mark the beginning of the end for the windmill. In the last one hundred years, the number of windmills in Holland has declined at an alarming rate. Prior to the mid-nineteenth century, nearly ten thousand windmills graced the landscape of this tiny country. By the beginning of the twentieth century, only twenty-five hundred windmills remained. In the 1920s, campaigns were initiated to preserve mills, but it was a difficult effort because the structures were regarded as commonplace and old-fashioned compared to the new attractions of steam power and electricity. In the 1970s, fewer than one thousand windmills remained, on account of neglect and the ravages of war.

Holland is known the world over for its spectacular tulips and incomparable windmills.
Here, the two unite to create an image that every visitor to Holland savors and remembers.

Above: Sheep graze before giant smock mills in Leidschendam, Holland. This imposing row of powerful windmills characterizes the landscape of the Netherlands. Opposite: Windmills and water form a perfect marriage in Holland. In this country, wherever there are dikes, lakes, and canals, there are also windmills. Pages 64-65: This post mill near Leiden, Holland, forms an integral part of the rural landscape. The entire upper body of a post mill turns along with the sails, while the post on the lower level remains stationary.

Today, the Dutch government and such organizations as the Dutch Windmill Society and the Guild of Volunteer Millers work to preserve these handsome giants, and regulations prohibit their destruction. A windmill museum in central Holland celebrates the heritage of these national landmarks. Currently, about half the surviving windmills in Holland are privately owned, and the other half lie in the hands of preservation soci-eties. Some have been turned into museums, homes, weekend cottages, or restaurants; others are simply landmarks. There are about 150 millers in Holland today, though many work only part-time or as a hobby. As they have for centuries, windmills continue to beautify the Dutch landscape and mirror the determination and practicality of the Dutch people, who won their land from the sea through hard work, ingenuity, and windmills.

The Language of Windmills

Before the days of mass communication, townsfolk relied on any means at hand to get information. In many towns, windmills were at least as tall as church towers, and the windmill provided a creative medium for broadcasting news to the surrounding village. Traditionally, millers positioned the sails of their mills to convey certain messages, such as whether or not the miller was in, the fact that there was a death in town, or news of a wedding or other celebration. In this way, the windmill acted like a billboard or newspaper for everyone who could see it.

A complex language developed in Holland, where it became customary to convey messages via windmill. The sails could be used to warn of floods or weak dikes, for example. A sail in the "going" position—just past its highest point—might signal the death of someone in the town. Boards could be removed from the sails, or the canvas sails themselves could be manipulated. If the miller himself died, crossboards were removed and the arms turned slowly to follow the body to its final resting place during the funeral. The windmill might stay in this position for weeks, except when the wind rose and there was work to be done.

Good news could also be conveyed by the windmill. A sail in a "coming" position—in which one of the arms stopped just short of its highest point—might signal the birth of a child, a marriage, or a birthday. Decorations such as flowers or banners, garlands, or coats of arms could be added to the sails during these events.

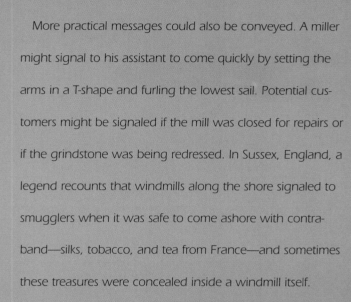

More practical messages could also be conveyed. A miller might signal to his assistant to come quickly by setting the arms in a T-shape and furling the lowest sail. Potential customers might be signaled if the mill was closed for repairs or if the grindstone was being redressed. In Sussex, England, a legend recounts that windmills along the shore signaled to smugglers when it was safe to come ashore with contraband—silks, tobacco, and tea from France—and sometimes these treasures were concealed inside a windmill itself.

This language proved particularly useful during wartime. When the British captured Nantucket Island during the American Revolutionary War, the islanders set the sails of their famous windmill to signal their ships at sea not to come in. This kept the sailors from falling into a trap, and the British waited in vain for the boats to come into the harbor. This practice has persisted into the twentieth century. During World War II, when Holland was occupied by German troops, underground and Allied pilots were sent messages via the language of windmills. Allied pilots who crashed in Holland were assisted by members of the Dutch underground, who were signaled by the code of the sails.

The windmills of Kinderdijk, Holland, express the monumentality inherent in Dutch windmills. They stand like icons of the nation.

*Gazing upon this scene, which features a lineup of windmills and a medieval castle in the
Spanish province of La Mancha, one can easily imagine the inspiration for Cervantes'* Don Quixote.

Windmills of the Plains and the Seas

Although Holland led the way in the sheer numbers and specialization of its windmills, these wondrous creations extended beyond the Netherlands throughout the European continent and the British Isles. France and Germany boasted many types of windmills, but England is second only to Holland in the number of windmills that dotted the landscape in centuries past. By 1750, the skyline of London was filled with windmills, with one for every square mile (2.6sq km) of the city. Like Holland, the city of London was surrounded by marshlands, and the mills made the environs habitable as the city expanded. London's streets even had names like Mill Wall and Windmill Street.

England was also home to a number of highly unusual windmills. An inventive millwright constructed a unique mill in Battersea to process linseed oil and malt. It was a great contraption with sails on the *interior* of the building, protected by rows of ninety-six shutters. The shutters could be opened like venetian blinds when the wind picked up to turn the sails. The immense yet odd building was nearly one hundred forty feet (42m) tall and fifty-four feet (16m) across. A local story tells of a Russian emperor who fancied the church of Battersea so much that he wished to take it back home with him and con-

Above: *An unusual white windmill stands in a field in Norfolk, England. Many people don't realize that at one time England boasted nearly as many windmills as Holland.*
Opposite: *Located in Avonshire, Somerset, the Stembridge Tower Mill is the last stand-ing thatched-roof windmill of southern England. In England and around the world, windmill preservation societies work to maintain these historic structures.*

structed a giant "carrying case" for it; but the villagers would not let their church go, so the great carrying case stayed in place.

Windmills fascinated artists and writers of Great Britain. The painter John Constable, like Rembrandt, was the son of a miller and was raised in a windmill; it's not surprising that windmills were commonly featured in his paintings. Constable had a model of a windmill in his studio, and it is even reported that he died while painting his favorite subject.

The famous writer and poet Robert Louis Stevenson, author of *Treasure Island*, wrote that he knew of:

> *few merrier spectacles than that of many windmills bickering together in a fresh breeze in a woody country; their halting alacrity of movement, their pleasant business, making bread all day long with uncouth gesticulations, their air, gigantically human, as of a creature half alive.*

Above: *England boasts some enormous windmills, including this one in Norfolk. Dutch and English windmills sometimes reached five or six stories.*
Opposite: *This charming mill is in Oland Island, Sweden. One of the windiest regions on earth, Scandinavia is home to many windmills.*
Today, Scandinavian scientists stand at the vanguard of the latest developments in windmill technology.

In Essex, England, an historic mill known as "John Webb's windmill" stands tall in a wheatfield. Grinding wheat was one of the principal tasks of windmills in past centuries.

The late eighteenth- and early nineteenth-century author William Cobbett was particularly impressed by the sight of seventeen windmills in one place:

> *Their twirling together added greatly to the beauty of the scene, which, having the broad and beautiful arm of the sea on one hand, and fields and meadows, studded with farm houses, on the other, appeared to be the most beautiful sight of the kind that I had ever beheld.*

In the 1600s, English taverns served beer to their customers in delightful "windmill cups." On one side of each cup was a tiny windmill with sails that would twirl if the drinker blew into a tube. The cups had rounded bottoms that would cause a spill unless the drinker finished his drink before replacing it on the bar.

In spite of the illustrious heritage of English windmills, and their great numbers in centuries past, only about one hundred survive today. A few, such as the North Leverton mill in Nottingham, still grind grain that is sold to tourists to finance the mill's upkeep. The Society for the Protection of Ancient Buildings endeavors to preserve the country's few remaining examples of traditional windmills.

As one of the windiest regions of the world, Scandinavia is also home to many windmills. In the Åland Islands of Finland, for example, nine hundred post mills survive, built from the plentiful trees in the area. Today, scientists in Finland and Denmark stand at the forefront of windmill innovation. Jutland, on the coast of Denmark, has become one of the world's leading testing grounds for experimental wind machines.

Windmills of the Mediterranean

Spain, Portugal, Italy, Turkey, and Greece boast large numbers of windmills that are distinct in style from those of northern Europe. These windmills bring rustic beauty to a new level, celebrating the simplicity and diversity of vernacular architecture. Mediterranean windmills are usually smaller than their enormous counterparts in Holland. Triangular jib sails are characteristic of windmills of the Mediterranean, and these bright white,

This windmill in Yulikavak, Turkey, shares a common ancestry with the windmills of other Mediterranean countries, including Spain and Greece.

cloth sails bring to mind sailing ships moored in the protected harbors of these sea-loving countries.

By the time Cervantes wrote his famous *Don Quixote* in the seventeenth century, windmills had long been a common sight in Spain. Windmills may have appeared on the Iberian Peninsula with the arrival of the Moors from North Africa as early as the eighth century. In fact, the Moors established Europe's first paper mill—which was powered by the wind— at Játiva, on Spain's southern coast. In Portugal, some millers exploited the musical potential of the wind by attaching terra-cotta pots to the arms of the windmills to make them wail as the arms turned. The pitch would indicate to the miller the speed of the sails.

Above: *Homemade windmills such as this one—located on the Lassithi Plateau on the Greek island of Crete—play an important role in local agriculture.* Right: *The white, thatched-roof windmills of Mykonos have long greeted visitors to the Greek island. From the sea, these structures loom large and help account for the unique quality of the island.*

This windmill in Karpathos, on the Dodecanese Islands of Greece, uses the small, jib-shaped sails typical of windmills in the Mediterranean region.

The tiny sails of this windmill on the island of Mykonos, Greece, are furled around its arms. Though the average European windmill had about four sails, some had as few as two and others as many as eight or more.

In the Greek islands, windmills are often clustered in groups or lined up like soldiers along the shoreline. Many of these are small, whitewashed stone towers with sharply pointed roofs and up to a dozen triangular jib sails. On Crete, for example, the tower mills, built of blinding white stucco with thatched roofs, display a dozen small sails circulating in the breeze. The mills of the Greek isles are relatively small compared to their northern neighbors, measuring about fifty feet (15m) in diameter. The picturesque island of Mykonos boasts some of the most striking windmills of the Mediterranean. Most of these are small and in private hands, and have been operating as long as anyone can remember.

Above: *The famous windmills that stand along the harbor of the Greek island of Rhodes have beckoned to sailors, explorers, and Crusaders for centuries.*
Opposite: *The windmills of Consuegra, in the Spanish province of La Mancha, stand along a windy ridge. Monuments such as these have graced the Iberian peninsula since the Middle Ages.*

Until electricity became more available to more villages and rural areas in the 1960s, about ten thousand windmills pumped water on mainland Greece and its many surrounding islands. These clusters of mills seemed to foretell modern "wind farms," in which towering turbines align in rows as far as the eye can see.

Don Quixote's Windmills

*I*n Cervantes' ironic tale *Don Quixote*, the protagonist—the hero and dreamer Don Quixote—is so enamored with old stories of fair maidens and brave knights that he decides to engage in chivalry himself. An old, bony nag named Rosinante becomes his steed; a plump farm girl becomes his fair maiden and the object of his affection; a farmhand becomes his squire. A group of windmills becomes a menacing race of giants that the self-styled knight sets out to slay. When he stabs at one of these "giants," the first sail launches his lance heavenward and the second launches Don Quixote off his horse. "These giants have been changed into windmills," he complains, vowing revenge. The windmills Don Quixote battles must have been similar to the ones that dot the Iberian Peninsula today. Most Spanish windmills were low constructions built of stone, with conical roofs and wide cloth sails.

Since Cervantes penned *Don Quixote* around 1605-1615, the phrase "tilting at windmills" has slipped into common language. The phrase has come down from Golden Age Spain to twentieth-century slang and is used to describe engaging an imaginary opponent or threat in conflict. It also can be used metaphorically to describe someone who is chasing an unrealistic dream.

These windmills in the Spanish province of La Mancha may not look very different from those Cervantes had in mind when he wrote his famous tale, Don Quixote.

Above: *On the Iberian peninsula, some millers attached terra-cotta pots to the arms of windmills such as this one in Peniche, Portugal, making music with unique instruments.* Opposite: *On the island of Majorca, Spain, the old stones of this six-armed windmill speak volumes about the centuries-old heritage of the windmill in Mediterranean countries.* Pages 86-87: *This windmill stands in an expansive park known as the Bois de Boulogne, located on the edge of modern Paris.*

Windmills once covered the entire European continent from Scandinavia to Greece. They took many forms, from the simple post mill to tower and smock mills, and later metal-vaned mills like this one in Majorca, Spain.

Standing against a crimson sky in Belmont, Texas, the metal-framed
North American windmill stands as a monument to pioneer ingenuity.

Windmills of the Cities and the Farms

When European explorers arrived in the New World, one of their first tasks was constructing windmills. Legend has it that on his third voyage, Christopher Columbus brought along a millwright and grindstone so that mills could be built in the West Indies. But crops in the New World were different from those back home, and mills were soon adapted to the task of crushing sugarcane, one of the major resources of the Caribbean. Not surprisingly, the places the Dutch settled—including the Dutch West Indies, Java, and South Africa—soon were populated by windmills, which served as practical machines as well as symbols of wealth and colonial power.

Windmills in the New York Skyline

It's hard to imagine, but by the 1600s, windmills formed landmarks in the skyline of New York City. Dutch colonists constructed these first "skyscrapers," which were still visible in the nineteenth century in lower Manhattan. In these early days, New York (which was then called New Amsterdam) resembled an old Dutch seaport rather than the bustling modern metropolis it would later become. Breukelen—a farming community later known as Brooklyn—also boasted a windmill used for grinding corn in that era.

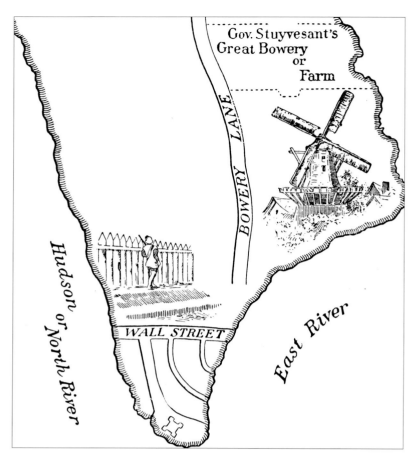

This 1660 map of the lower tip of the island of Manhattan, featuring the settlement called New Amsterdam, shows two items one might not expect to find in New York City: a farm and a windmill. Dutch settlers constructed several windmills there in the seventeenth century.

The Windmill Belt

Windmills arrived in North America with the earliest settlers. The French built mills in Canada, and the English on the coast of the American colonies. Until windmills were outmoded in the late 1800s, the United States had a "windmill belt" that extended from the eastern tip of Long Island northward through Rhode Island, Cape Cod, and Nantucket. The proliferation of windmills along these rocky shores must have formed a picturesque scene that could rival any European port.

The first windmill built in the colonies was erected on Cape Cod shortly after settlers arrived at Plymouth Rock. Windmills occupied nearly every elevated point on the peninsula, and many of these were used to process salt from pumping seawater. Seawater was pumped into large vats and evaporated on sunny days, leaving a deposit of salt. Until the middle of the nineteenth century, nearly all the salt consumed in the United States came from Cape Cod. Once the duty on foreign salt was reduced and salt could be purchased more cheaply from sources outside the country, the industry was gradually abandoned.

New York's first windmill was erected in the early 1600s in lower Manhattan behind the fort at the Battery and belonged to the Dutch West India Company. Ferrymen used the mill as a weather vane. If the sails were furled, a storm was brewing and they would refuse to carry passengers across the East River. Abraham Pietersen, a Dutch miller, had moved from his native Haarlem to America to run the mill at the Battery. Pietersen was renowned for his boisterous temper, for which he was brought before a judge several times. More mills were constructed later throughout the city, including the Garrison Windmill, located farther north on Manhattan Island. Cortlandt Street was once called Old Windmill Lane after the mill that stood there.

Long Island boasted many windmills built by English settlers, and some of the country's oldest windmills survive there. Suffolk County on Long Island has one of the highest concentrations of seventeenth- and eighteenth-century windmills in the United States. Some of these are smock mills, and others are deemed "petticoat mills" because of the decorative caps that reminded townsfolk of women's petticoats. The oldest surviving mill—known as the Mill Hill Mill—stands in Southhampton and was built at the turn of the eighteenth century.

*Atop a grassy knoll on Ile-aux-Coudres in the Canadian province of Quebec sits a windmill, or
"moulin a vent" to the French-speaking citizens of the region. Built in 1830, this stone windmill
has withstood over a century and a half of wind and weather.*

*On Long Island, New York, stands the Old Hook Wind Mill. Long Island boasts the largest group of standing historic windmills
in the United States. Many of them are tower mills, based on new settlers' memories of European precedents.*

The windmills of New England—like this smock mill in Eastham, Massachusetts—are among the oldest in the United States.

These coastal windmills, which were based on European models, served the function of both lighthouse and weather vane for ships at sea. Captains of sailing vessels had only to look ashore toward the windmills to know which direction to point their own sails. Many posters placed at ferry docks read "Operates daily except when the windmill lowers its sails."

A Midwestern Landmark

Until they were replaced with electricity from the 1930s onward, windmills in North America ensured the livelihood and even the survival of farmers on the plains and in the Southwest. As soon as settlers began moving west after the Civil War, the need for adequate water supplies to support farming became apparent.

Above: *The raising of domestic livestock would have proven impossible in arid western and midwestern North America if it weren't for the steadfast work of the windmill.* Below: *Across the North American continent, homemade windmills solve practical problems and delight the eye. This windmill/whirligig was constructed with bicycle wheels and tin cups.*

Although there was plenty of fertile land to go around, water to feed livestock and irrigate crops was in short supply. Windmills were built to draw water from wells deep within the ground. Since few other water sources were available, windmills made inhospitable lands fit for habitation and farming.

Rather than grinding grain or performing other tasks that steam power had long since replaced, the water-pumping windmill on the North American plains was perfectly suited for the midwestern farmer. There was no need to erect a large tower of the type found in Europe or New England; this would have been prohibitive to the practical-minded, penny-pinching farmer. Instead, all that was required was a frame and wooden vanes. This form was light enough to be easily transported, yet sturdy enough to withstand the harsh winds that whipped the plains. The form was standardized in the 1850s by Daniel Halladay, a machinist, and John Burnham, who was in the pump business. It was much smaller than European windmills but was well suited to the needs of the midwestern rancher and farmer. Its design would not change for one hundred years.

The traditional midwestern windmill used a revolving shaft—like a big spiral or screw—bored into an underground water source that lifted water out of the ground and funneled it into a vat or other repository. Windmill designers determined that many small blades were better at catching the wind than four big ones, so the vanes resemble a fan. This invention was a boon to farmers who had no other way to bring water to their crops and livestock in this arid area. These windmill pumps supplied water for feed troughs, irrigated fields, and refilled locomotive tanks.

The job of these windmills in Araruma County, Brazil, is salt extraction. Their form—identical to that of the windmills of the western United States—spread across North and South America, as well as to developing nations around the world in the twentieth century.

By the 1880s, wooden vanes were replaced with steel, and the base also was fashioned out of metal. This small, lightweight model could easily be shipped by train, ship, or wagon and could pump water from a well of any depth. An average ranch might have ten to fifteen windmills, though bigger estates might have as many as one hundred. Each mill could be as large as fifty feet (15m) in diameter and as high as eighty feet (24m) tall. By 1900, the flatlands teemed with whirring windmills.

In the Midwest, windmill builders made a good living traveling around, and the machines were also available by mail order. Cattle hands could supplement their wrangling income if they had some mechanical skill. Jake Friesen, a windmill builder, built four thousand windmills in twenty-five years across Kansas and Oklahoma, and his children followed in his footsteps. Between the 1880s and 1930s, about 6.5 million windmills were constructed in the United States, and many were shipped from Chicago, the windmill manufacturing hub of the nation.

The American windmill—recognizable by its skeletal frame of steel girders, topped by sheet metal sails or vanes—was easily transferred to Argentina, which supports a large meat industry and where cowboys drive herds from one watering hole to another. Windmills were transported in boatloads from the United States to South America, where they soon became a ubiquitous feature of the landscape. Likewise, the American-style windmill accounted for the workability of the Australian outback and the settling of many areas that had remained desolate on that continent. Similar windmills have been put to work in South Africa and in developing nations around the world to bring water to areas that have little or none.

On Salt Cay in the Turks and Caicos Islands of the Caribbean, dusk falls on the salt ponds, and the silhouette of a small windmill emerges against the waning blue sky. Pages 100-101: *Windmills such as this metal-framed one were as integral a part of farming and ranching in the American old West as wood fences and barbed wire. Windmills enabled farmers and ranchers to extract scarce water from the ground and provide for their crops and cattle.*

Above: *Necessity is the mother of invention: early North American farmers moving west needed reliable water supplies for their crops and livestock. This old windmill and building stand in the Cabeza Prieta National Wildlife Refuge in Arizona.*
Opposite: *When Europeans settled in the New World, they brought along their traditions of windmill-building. It's no surprise that many of the earliest windmills of North America and the West Indies resemble their European ancestors.*

In Mount Dora, Minnesota, the setting sun forms the background for a traditional midwestern-style American windmill.
Made of wood and later steel, these mills became common features of the American landscape.

Above: *A futuristic-looking wind generator towers over the desert landscape of Palm Springs, California, where this contemporary windmill harnesses energy for the community.* Pages 106-107: *A dilapidated barn and old metal windmill stand in contrast to golden-hued corn stalks, creating a picturesque scene. The dry prairies that water from windmills originally made into rich farmland still thrive as the breadbasket of the world.*

Today, midwestern-style windmills survive as rusted, creaky reminders of a rich farming heritage. North America boasts some impressive windmill collections, and the number of private collectors of these historical artifacts continues to rise. One collector in New Mexico has amassed the largest private collection of windmills in the United States. More than sixty antique windmills, most dating from between 1870 and 1930, cover the twenty-acre (8ha) estate of the collector.

Windmills of Today

Though they declined in use from the 1920s, windmills regained popularity in North America—and indeed around the world—during the 1970s. To halt depletion of the earth's supply of natural resources—coal, petroleum, natural gas, and other limited fossil fuels—people began to look for ways to use energy sources that are unlimited and free; the wind fits that bill. The movement continues to gain momentum as we enter the twenty-first century and scientists continue to test wind turbines and other wind machines around the world for solutions to our planet's ever-changing energy challenges. Whether or not windmills hold the key to energy solutions of the future, their illustrious past guarantees a premier place for them in the history of architecture, technology, and humanity.

Left: *This steel pump mill in Illinois stands as a reminder of the importance of windmills in the rural life of the American midwest.* Below: *High on the Altamont Pass in California, towering wind machines and cattle cohabitate.*

Windmills of the Future

Windmills have always been monuments of innovation, used to solve many problems, from grinding grain to pumping water. Today, the history of windmills is charting a new course. Fossil fuels, such as coal and oil, are in shorter supply, and engineers and conservationists have returned to wind power as a generator of energy. Engineers are currently designing innovative, experimental machines. Countries at the cutting edge of windmill development include Denmark and the United States. These advanced windmills are subject to a new aesthetic. Instead of the old-world charm and picturesque quality of the historic windmills, stark, even severe-looking, metal contraptions appear in the fields. But these high-tech creations let us appreciate their raw engineering and functionality.

Not all windmill experiments have met with success. In the 1930s at Grandpa's Knob, a windy, two-thousand-foot (608m) -high mountain peak near Rutland, Vermont, a group of engineers set out to build the world's largest windmill. After five years of research and the work of more than

two hundred scientists, they created a 110-foot (33m) metal tower with a twin-blade rotor and a huge metal egg containing generating equipment that spun around like a traditional windmill. It ran flawlessly for a year, but then one of the parts failed. It took two years to replace the part on account of metal rationing during World War II, and ran for only a month before one of the sails broke off, flew through the air, and landed. It was never repaired, and the project was soon abandoned.

With the depletion of the world's fossil fuels, a quest for efficient energy, and a desire to reduce pollution, countries around the world have developed windmills for specific applications. From India to Morocco to Denmark, windmills are being developed to address the energy challenges of the future, and we may yet witness a day when the windmill regains its position as a premier tool for generating energy from the wind.

The expansive, windy landscape of California has served as the testing ground for new windmill experiments. In the Tehachapi Mountains, a wind farm consisting of stark, futuristic wind turbines generates energy.

From Scandinavia to Australia, scientists continue to develop windmill technology. During the North American energy crisis of the 1970s, many people heralded windmills as a clean energy source that would not deplete the world's natural resources.

A lone windmill stands along the highway in sandhill country. Utilitarian but noble, windmills such as these dot the countryside.

Above: *In a stark landscape in the heartland of the United States, a lone windmill stands guard like a sentry.*
Ranchers and cowboys depended on these metal structures to pump water in the arid Midwest.
Opposite: *Cattle-raising would have proved impossible in some areas if it weren't for the many windmills,*
like this one in southern New Mexico, that pumped water from deep within the earth.

What is the fate of the world's historic windmills? Whether gracing the prairies of Canada or the countryside of Holland, these intriguing monuments deserve to be preserved for future generations.

Bibliography

Baker, T. Lindsay. *A Field Guide to American Windmills*. Norman, OK.: University of Oklahoma Press, 1985.

Barbour, Erwin Hinckley. "The Homemade Windmills of Nebraska," *Scientific American Supplement*, XLIV (January 13-27, 1900) 20098-20100, 20114-15, 20130-32.

Batten, M.I. *English Windmills*. London: Architectural Press, 1930-32.

Brown, Joseph, and Anne Ensign Brown. *Harness the Wind: The Story of Windmills*. New York: Dodd & Mead Co., 1977.

Cosner, Sharon. *American Windmills: Harnessers of Energy*. New York: David McKay Company, 1977.

Cross, Mike. *Wind Power*. New York: Gloucester Press, n.d.

Dennis, Landt. *Catch the Wind: A Book of Windmills and Windpower*. New York: Four Winds Press, 1976.

Eldridge, Frank R. *Wind Machines*. New York: Litton Educational Publishing, 1980.

Hamilton, Roger. "Can We Harness the Wind?" *National Geographic*, CXLVIII (December 1975) 812-28.

Hopkins, R.T., and S. Freese. *In Search of English Windmills*. London: Cecil Palmer Publishing Company, 1931.

Levine, Carol. "The Windmills of Long Island," *Early American Life*, V (February 1974) 24-27.

McDonald, Lucile. *Windmills: An Old-New Energy Source*. New York: Elsevier-Dutton, 1981.

Putnam, P.C. *Power from the Wind*. New York: Van Nostrand Reinhold, 1948.

Reynolds, John. *Windmills and Watermills*. New York: Praeger Publications, 1970.

Stokhuyzen, Frederick. *The Dutch Windmill*. New York: Praeger Publications, 1970.

Torrey, Volta. *Wind-Catchers: American Windmills of Yesterday and Tomorrow*. Brattleboro, Vt.: The Stephen Greene Press, 1976.

Wailes, Rex. *English Windmills*. London: Routledge and Kegan Paul, 1954.

Index

Photography Credits

©Howard Ande: pp. 104-105

Art Resource: ©Erich Lessing: pp. 36-37

©Barrett & Mackay Photography: p. 93

©Willard Clay: pp. 44-45, 90-91, 100-101, 103, 108 top, 114, back endpaper

©Dennie Cody: pp. 18-19, 25

©Richard Cummins: pp. 9, 27, 105 right

©John Elk III: p. 54 left

FPG, Int'l: pp. 21, 32 bottom, 33, 39, 41, 46-47; ©David Bartruff: pp. 76-77; ©Walter Bibikow: p. 81; ©Dennie Cody: p. 45 right; ©Gerald French: pp. 108-109; ©Eduardo Garcia: p. 97; ©Guy Marche: p. 102; ©Buddy Mays: pp. 110-111; ©David Noble: pp. 64-65, 112; ©Richard Price: p. 115; ©Travelpix: pp. 66-67, 88-89; ©Toyohiro Yamada: p. 50

©Winston Fraser: p. 24

©Chuck Haney: p. 16

Leo deWys, Inc.: pp. 30-31, 38; ©Charles Bowman: p. 71; ©Paul Gerda: pp. 6-7, 54-55; Jon Hicks: p. 70; ©Arthur Hustwitt: pp. 2, 75, 80; ©Henryk Kaiser: p. 94; ©Bob Krist: pp. 98-99; ©Jean-Paul Nacivet: pp. 86-87; ©Witold Skrypczak: pp. 82-83; ©Bas van Beek: p. 58; ©Steve Vidler: pp. 60-61, 62, 68-69, 73, 76 left, 85

Midwestock: ©Kevin Anderson: p. 116; ©Richard Day: pp. 106-107

New England Stock Photos: ©Marc A. Auth: p. 52 left; ©Lou Palmieri: p. 95; ©Kevin Shields: p. 42

North Wind Photo Archives: pp. 15, 22 both, 26, 43 both, 92

©Dan Polin: p. 96 bottom

Scope: ©Jacques Guillard: pp. 28-29

©Stock Montage, Inc.: pp. 23, 32 top, 35 right, 36 left,

©SuperStock: pp. 12-13, 14, 20, 34-35, 40, 56-57, 59, 63, 72, 78, 79, 84

©Tom Till: p. 96 top

Tony Stone Images: ©Gavin Hellier: pp. 48-49; ©Patrick Ingrand: p. 74; ©Jean-Paul Manceau: p. 8; ©G. Ryan & S. Beyer: p. 113; ©Jeremy Walker: p. 17, front endpaper

©Nance S. Trueworthy: p. 51

©Craig Wood: pp. 52-53

Woodfin Camp & Associates, Inc.: ©Robert Frerck: pp. 10-11

WITHDRAWN

LONGWOOD PUBLIC LIBRARY
3 0641 00162 5107